CREATED BY JENNIFER BAKER

Published by Wild Child Literacy

ISBN: 978-1-7381693-3-7

Wild Child Literacy is committed to creating nature connections by publishing stories and educational resources that nurture the wild child within us all.

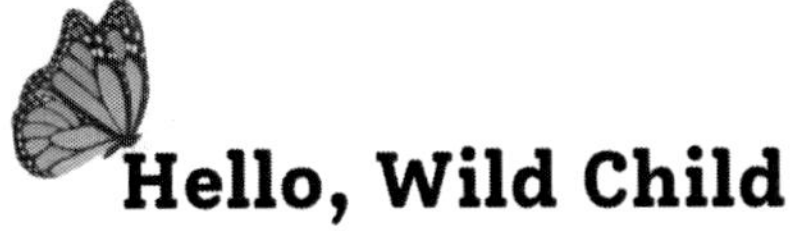

Hello, Wild Child

If you're reading this, it means you are ready for the outdoors—adventure, exercise, fresh air—nature is the perfect setting to blend exploration with education!

Sure, you can sit at a desk studying science while you gaze out the window, counting down the minutes until recess, but that sounds boring. And you, most definitely, are not boring. You're an explorer! So get outside, bring a friend (or ten), and go wild! Climb that massive boulder, balance your way across the fallen log, and leap over a babbling brook, all while observing, drawing, and asking questions about the wild world around you. What are you waiting for? Go. Explore. Learn. But, most importantly, stay wild, child!

Hello, Parents and Educators

Now that we have covered the exploration portion, let's dive into the education component. While your child or student navigates their natural environment, they will also practice art and hone their writing skills with dedicated pages for drawing, recording field notes, and crafting a story about their experience—independently or utilizing available writing prompts. Other curricular competencies addressed through this nature journal include:

- Demonstrating a wonder and curiosity about the world,
- Experiencing and interpreting the local environment,
- Sorting and classifying data and information using drawings,
- Making predictions and simple inferences based on prior knowledge,
- Identifying questions to answer through scientific inquiry and
- Making observations aimed at identifying their questions about the natural world.

A Walk in Nature Journal: Recordings of a Wild Child encourages your child or student to observe, draw, document, ask questions about what they see, and conduct research. It contains famous quotes about nature, multiple choice questions designed to provide extended learning opportunities, species log sheets, and room to record observations for twenty nature walks.

When we encourage children to form connections with nature, we empower them to become stewards of the land. Thank you for placing value on outdoor education. You are giving this child a gift that keeps on giving.

Jennifer Baker,

Jen Baker

Wild Child Literacy

This Journal Belongs to a
WILD CHILD
by the Name of

Supply List

1. Journal & Art supplies
2. Bug net and Collection jar
3. Binoculars / Magnifying glass
4. Field Guides
5. Sit Pad
6. Backpack With Water & Snack
7. Camera
8. Hat / Sunscreen
9. Family & Friends
10. Plenty of wild curiosity

Wildlife Safety

When walking through the wilderness, it is important to be mindful of the fact that you will be sharing space with wildlife that may be in the area. Most wild animals prefer to avoid people. Even so, there are steps that you should take to make sure that you are able to enjoy nature safely.

- **Walk in groups and make noise**
- **Learn to identify signs of wildlife**
- **Never approach wildlife**
- **Observe wildlife from a safe distance**
- **If you encounter a wild animal, do not run**
- **Stay calm, and as a group back away slowly**

A Walk on the Wild Side

Date: ________________ **Time:** ________________

Location: ________________________________

Weather:

> In every walk with nature,
> one receives far more
> than he seeks.
>
> – John Muir

I see:	
I hear:	
I smell:	
I feel:	

Nature Log

Use this space to record something that catches your eye. Sketch, colour, make a leaf rubbing – go wild! Nothing in nature is perfect, so let your inner artist shine.

Field Notes

TAKE A WILD GUESS!
THE OLDEST TREE SPECIES IN THE WORLD IS THE BRISTLECONE PINE, PINUS LONGAEVA. THE OLDEST IS BELIEVED TO BE ALMOST
A) 100 YEARS
B) 500 YEARS
C) 1000 YEARS
D) 5000 YEARS

That's A Wild Story!

WRITE A STORY ABOUT TODAY'S
NATURE WALK.
OR, HERE'S A WILD IDEA!
IMAGINE METHUSELAH, THE WORLDS
OLDEST BRISTLECONE PINE, CAN
TALK. WHAT WOULD YOU ASK IT?

A Walk on the Wild Side

Date: ______________ Time: ______________

Location: ______________________________

Weather:

> Nature is the source of all true knowledge.
>
> – Leonardo da Vinci

I see:	
I hear:	
I smell:	
I feel:	

Nature Log

Use this space to record something that catches your eye. Sketch, colour, make a leaf rubbing - go wild! Nothing in nature is perfect, so let your inner artist shine.

Field Notes

TAKE A WILD GUESS!
NORTHERN LEOPARD FROGS SURVIVE WINTER BY ENTERING A HIBERNATION-LIKE STATE KNOWN AS
A) BRUMATION
B) TORPOR
C) REM SLEEP
D) LONG SLEEP SYNDROME

That's A Wild Story!

WRITE A STORY ABOUT TODAY'S NATURE WALK.
OR, HERE'S A WILD IDEA!
USE THIS SPACE TO WRITE DOWN ANY QUESTIONS THAT YOU HAVE ABOUT FROGS. EXAMPLE: HOW DO FROGS BREATH THROUGH THEIR SKIN?

A Walk on the Wild Side

Date: ____________ Time: ____________

Location: ______________________________

Weather:

> In the spring, at the end of the day, you should smell like dirt.
>
> – Margaret Atwood

I see:	
I hear:	
I smell:	
I feel:	

Nature Log

Use this space to record something that catches your eye. Sketch, colour, make a leaf rubbing – go wild! Nothing in nature is perfect, so let your inner artist shine.

Field Notes

TAKE A WILD GUESS!
CATERPILLARS HAVE SIMPLE EYES CALLED OCELLI THAT DETECT CHANGES IN LIGHT. HOW MANY EYES DO MOST CATERPILLARS HAVE?
A) 2
B) 12
C) 22
D) 32

That's A Wild Story!

WRITE A STORY ABOUT TODAY'S NATURE WALK.
OR, HERE'S A WILD IDEA!
RESEARCH AND DRAW THE LIFE CYCLE OF A BUTTERFLY.

A Walk on the Wild Side

Date: ______________ Time: ______________

Location: ______________________________

Weather:

"Keep your face to the sunshine and you cannot see a shadow.

– Helen Keller"

I see:	
I hear:	
I smell:	
I feel:	

Nature Log

Use this space to record something that catches your eye. Sketch, colour, make a leaf rubbing – go wild! Nothing in nature is perfect, so let your inner artist shine.

Field Notes

TAKE A WILD GUESS!
WHEN PREPARING FOR HIBERNATION, BEARS EAT APPROXIMATELY
A) 2000 CALORIES/DAY
B) 10,000 CALORIES/DAY
C) 20,000 CALORIES/DAY
D) 50,000 CALORIES/DAY

That's A Wild Story!

WRITE A STORY ABOUT TODAY'S NATURE WALK.
OR, HERE'S A WILD IDEA!
PRETEND YOU'RE A BEAR, AND CREATE A GROCERY LIST USING NATURAL FOOD SOURCES. REMEMBER, BEARS ARE OMNIVORES. THEY EAT BOTH PLANTS AND ANIMALS.

A Walk on the Wild Side

Date: ______________ **Time:** ______________

Location: ______________________________

Weather:

> If you truly love nature, you will find beauty everywhere.
>
> – Vincent Van Gogh

I see:	
I hear:	
I smell:	
I feel:	

Nature Log

Use this space to record something that catches your eye. Sketch, colour, make a leaf rubbing – go wild! Nothing in nature is perfect, so let your inner artist shine.

Field Notes

TAKE A WILD GUESS!
TO PROTECT ITS BRAIN, THIS BIRD SPECIES HAS A LONG TONGUE THAT ACTS AS A SHOCK ABSORBER.
A) CROW
B) BLUE JAY
C) CHICKADEE
D) WOODPECKER

That's A Wild Story!

WRITE A STORY ABOUT TODAY'S NATURE WALK.
OR, HERE'S A WILD IDEA!
SNAGS ARE STANDING DEAD TREES. THEY ATTRACT INSECTS THAT ANIMALS LIKE WOODPECKERS FEED ON. HOW ELSE DO SNAGS HELP WILDLIFE?

A Walk on the Wild Side

Date: ______________ Time: ______________

Location: ______________________________

Weather:

> Look deep into nature, and then you will understand everything better.
>
> – Albert Einstein

I see:	
I hear:	
I smell:	
I feel:	

Nature Log

Use this space to record something that catches your eye. Sketch, colour, make a leaf rubbing - go wild! Nothing in nature is perfect, so let your inner artist shine.

Field Notes

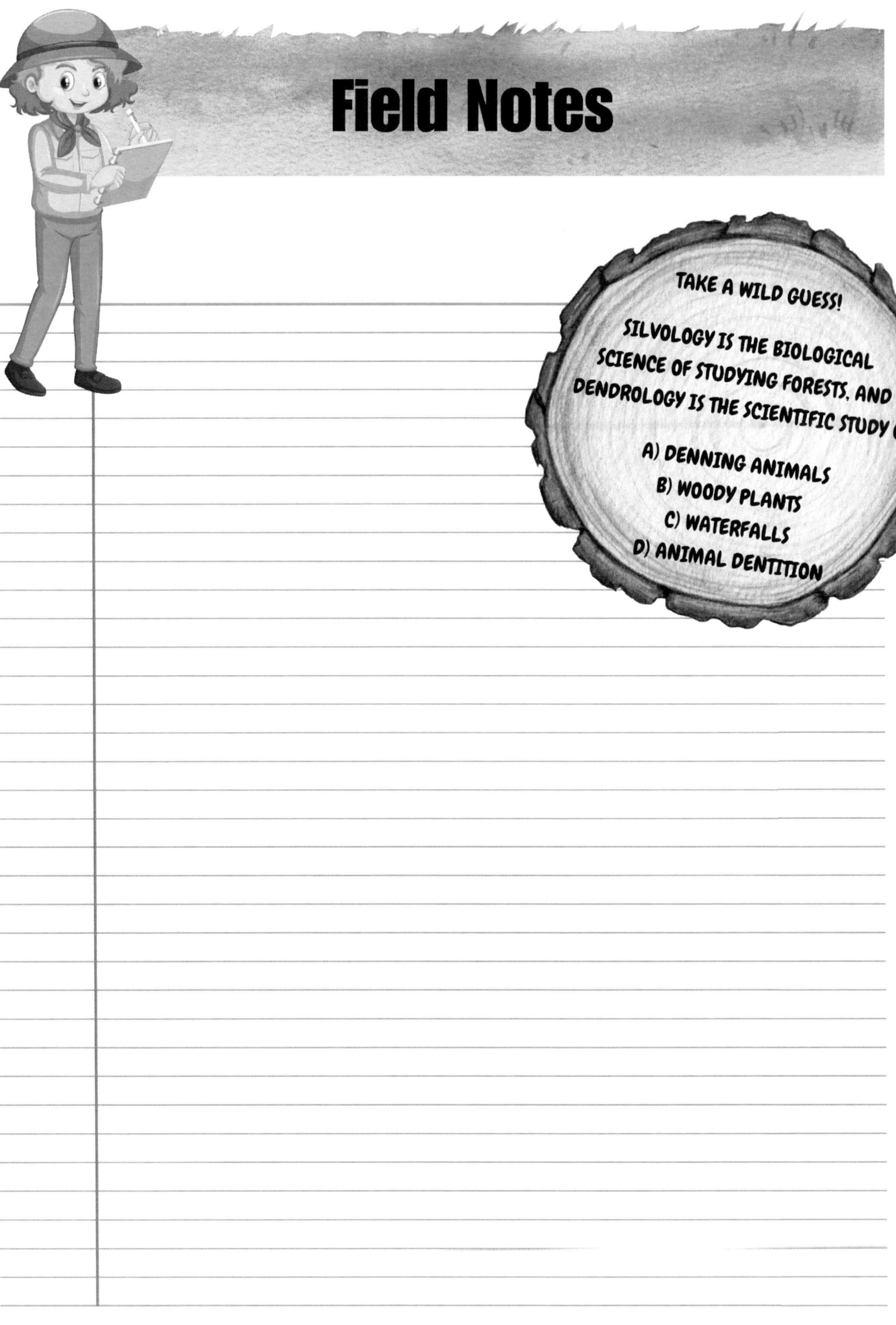
TAKE A WILD GUESS!
SILVOLOGY IS THE BIOLOGICAL SCIENCE OF STUDYING FORESTS, AND DENDROLOGY IS THE SCIENTIFIC STUDY OF
A) DENNING ANIMALS
B) WOODY PLANTS
C) WATERFALLS
D) ANIMAL DENTITION

That's A Wild Story!

WRITE A STORY ABOUT TODAY'S NATURE WALK.
OR, HERE'S A WILD IDEA!
DRAW YOUR FAVORITE KIND OF TREE, AND EXPLAIN WHY YOU LIKE IT.

A Walk on the Wild Side

Date: ____________ Time: ____________

Location: ______________________________

Weather:

> The earth has music for those who listen.
>
> – William Shakespeare

I see:	
I hear:	
I smell:	
I feel:	

Nature Log

Use this space to record something that catches your eye. Sketch, colour, make a leaf rubbing – go wild! Nothing in nature is perfect, so let your inner artist shine.

Field Notes

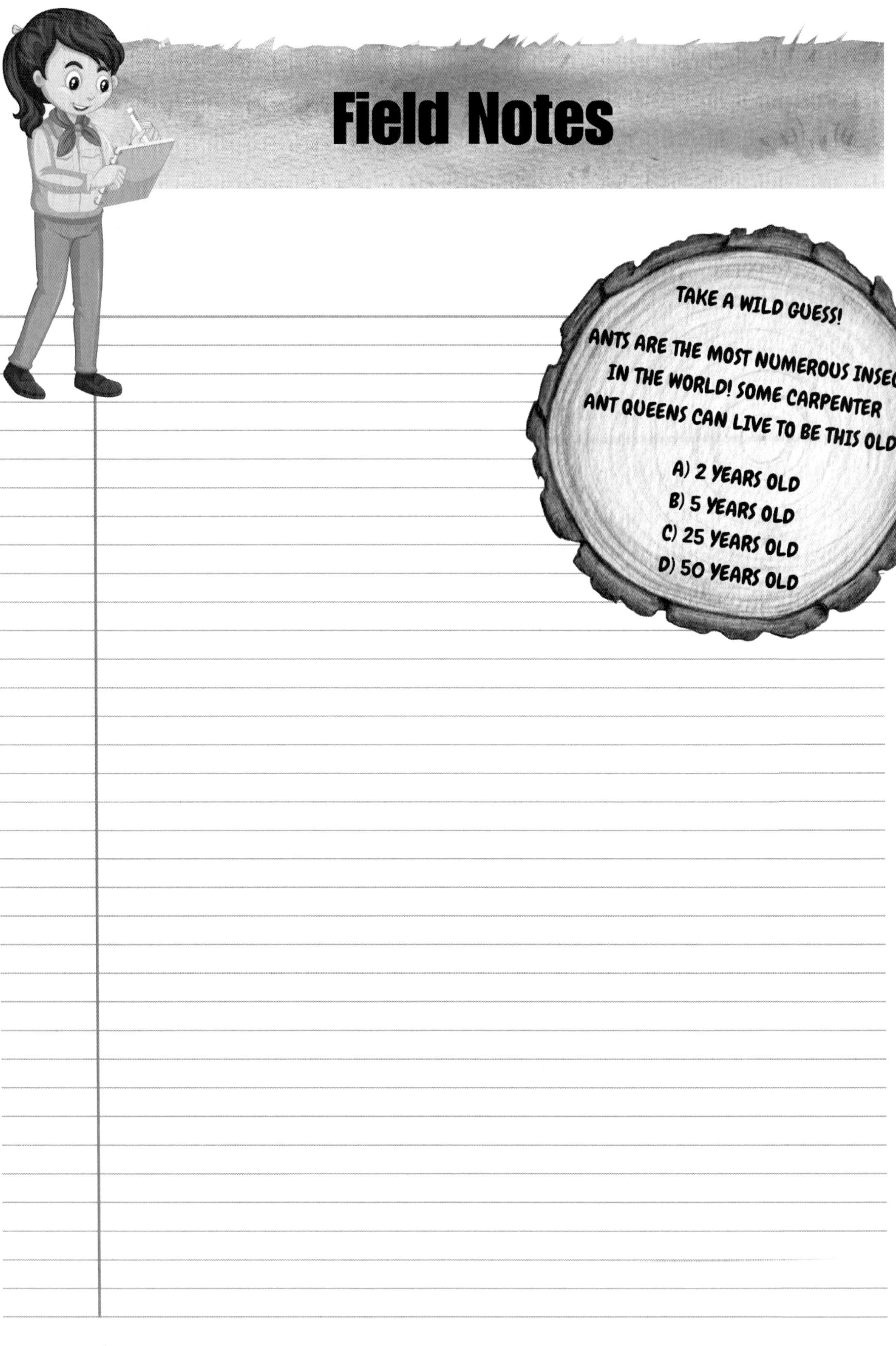
TAKE A WILD GUESS!
ANTS ARE THE MOST NUMEROUS INSECT IN THE WORLD! SOME CARPENTER ANT QUEENS CAN LIVE TO BE THIS OLD
A) 2 YEARS OLD
B) 5 YEARS OLD
C) 25 YEARS OLD
D) 50 YEARS OLD

That's A Wild Story!

WRITE A STORY ABOUT TODAY'S NATURE WALK.
OR, HERE'S A WILD IDEA!
IMAGINE YOU ARE A CARPENTER ANT.
DRAW A PICTURE OF YOUR UNDERGROUND HOME SHOWING ENTRANCES, TUNNELS, AND NEST SITES.

A Walk on the Wild Side

Date: ____________ Time: ____________

Location: ____________________________

Weather:

> All my life through, the new sights of nature made me rejoice like a child.
>
> – Marie Curie

I see:	
I hear:	
I smell:	
I feel:	

Nature Log

Use this space to record something that catches your eye.
Sketch, colour, make a leaf rubbing – go wild! Nothing in nature is perfect, so let your inner artist shine.

Field Notes

TAKE A WILD GUESS!
THIS ANIMAL HAS YELLOWISH TEETH BECAUSE THEIR ENAMEL CONTAINS IRON
A) ELK
B) MOOSE
C) BEAVER
D) COUGAR

That's A Wild Story!

WRITE A STORY ABOUT TODAY'S NATURE WALK.
OR, HERE'S A WILD IDEA!
BEAVERS BUILD LODGES. LIST OTHER TYPES OF HOMES USED BY WILDLIFE?

A Walk on the Wild Side

Date: ____________ Time: ____________

Location: ______________________________

Weather:

> The goal of life is living in agreement with nature.
>
> – Zeno

I see:	
I hear:	
I smell:	
I feel:	

Nature Log

Use this space to record something that catches your eye. Sketch, colour, make a leaf rubbing – go wild! Nothing in nature is perfect, so let your inner artist shine.

Field Notes

TAKE A WILD GUESS!
THE DIET OF "THIS" PREDATOR IS MADE UP OF ALMOST ENTIRELY SNOWSHOE HARES
A) LYNX
B) WOLF
C) COYOTE
D) BALD EAGLE

That's A Wild Story!

WRITE A STORY ABOUT TODAY'S NATURE WALK.
OR, HERE'S A WILD IDEA!
THE LYNX AND THE SNOWSHOE HARE HAVE A SYMBIOTIC RELATIONSHIP. WHAT ARE OTHER WILDLIFE SPECIES THAT HAVE ON-GOING CLOSE INTERACTIONS?

A Walk on the Wild Side

Date: ______________ Time: ______________

Location: ______________________________

Weather:

> Those who contemplate the beauty of earth find reserves of strength that will endure as long as life lasts.
>
> – Rachel Carson

I see:	
I hear:	
I smell:	
I feel:	

Nature Log

Use this space to record something that catches your eye. Sketch, colour, make a leaf rubbing - go wild! Nothing in nature is perfect, so let your inner artist shine.

Field Notes

TAKE A WILD GUESS!
OWLS ARE DIVIDED INTO TWO FAMILIES. STRIGIDAE, THE TRUE OWLS, AND
A) SCHOOL OWLS
B) BARN OWLS
C) HOUSE OWLS
D) NONE OF THE ABOVE

That's A Wild Story!

WRITE A STORY ABOUT TODAY'S NATURE WALK.
OR, HERE'S A WILD IDEA!
OWLS ARE NOCTURNAL, MEANING THEY ARE ACTIVE AT NIGHT.
NAME AN ADAPTATION THAT HELPS OWLS HUNT IN THE DARK.

Mammal Observation Log

Date	Species	Scientific Name	Quantity	Location

Bird Observation Log

Date	Species	Scientific Name	Quantity	Location

Reptile Observation Log

Date	Species	Scientific Name	Quantity	Location

Amphibian Observation Log

Date	Species	Scientific Name	Quantity	Location

Plant Observation Log

Date	Species	Scientific Name	Quantity	Location

Insect Observation Log

Date	Species	Scientific Name	Quantity	Location

Field Notes

Field Notes

Field Notes

Field Notes

A Walk on the Wild Side

Date: ______________ Time: ______________

Location: ______________________________

Weather:

> Nature is not a place to visit.
> It is home.
>
> – Gary Snyder

I see:	
I hear:	
I smell:	
I feel:	

Nature Log

Use this space to record something that catches your eye. Sketch, colour, make a leaf rubbing – go wild! Nothing in nature is perfect, so let your inner artist shine.

Field Notes

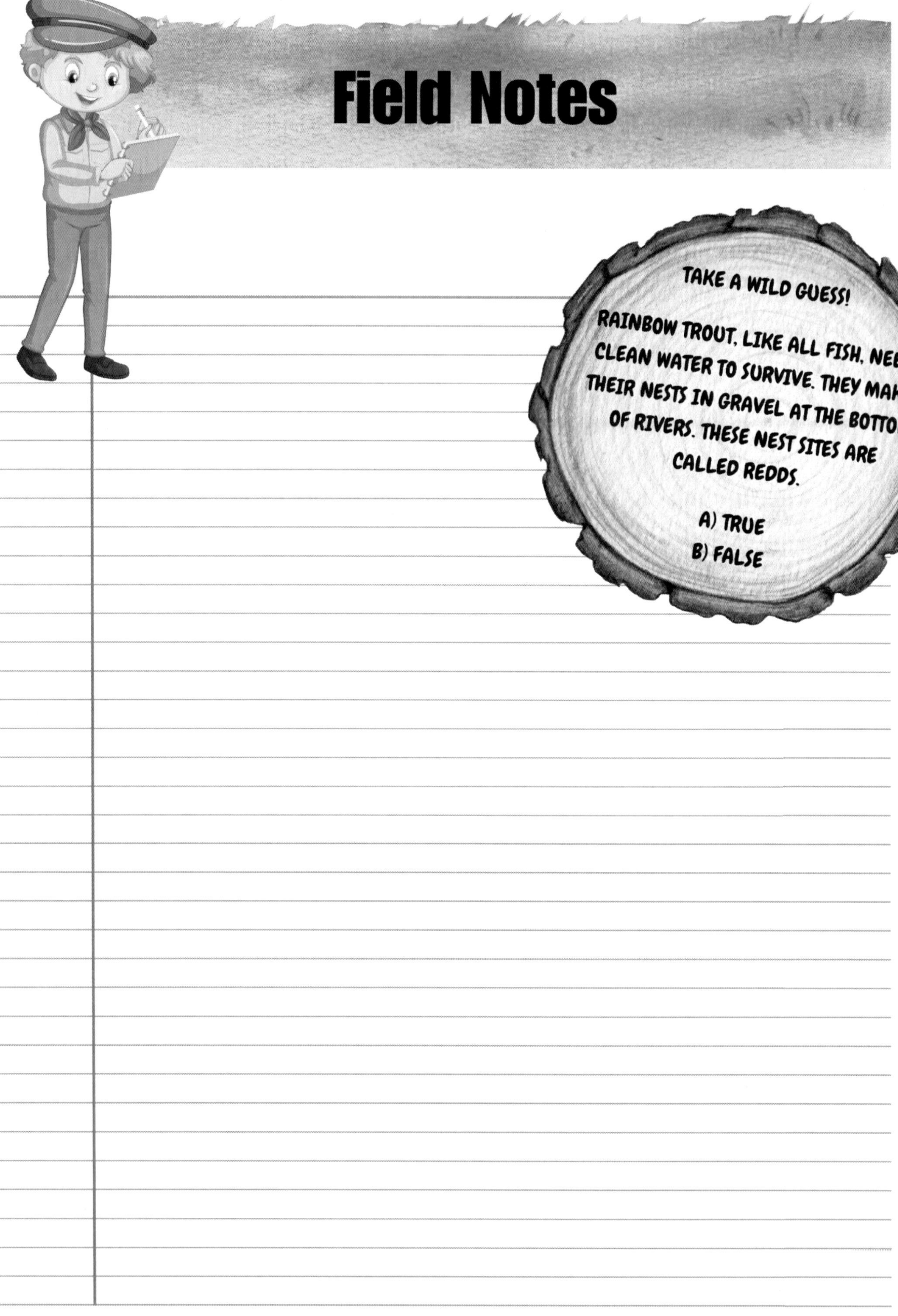
TAKE A WILD GUESS!
RAINBOW TROUT, LIKE ALL FISH, NEED CLEAN WATER TO SURVIVE. THEY MAKE THEIR NESTS IN GRAVEL AT THE BOTTOM OF RIVERS. THESE NEST SITES ARE CALLED REDDS.
A) TRUE
B) FALSE

That's A Wild Story!

WRITE A STORY ABOUT TODAY'S NATURE WALK.
OR, HERE'S A WILD IDEA!
DRAW A RAINBOW TROUT, AND LABEL THE EYE, MOUTH, GILL COVER, LATERAL LINE, AND FINS (DORSAL, ADIPOSE, CAUDAL, ANAL, PELVIC, & PECTORAL).

A Walk on the Wild Side

Date: ______________ Time: ______________

Location: ______________________________

Weather:

> The land knows you,
> even when you are lost.
>
> – Robin Wall Kimmerer

I see:	
I hear:	
I smell:	
I feel:	

Nature Log

Use this space to record something that catches your eye. Sketch, colour, make a leaf rubbing - go wild! Nothing in nature is perfect, so let your inner artist shine.

Field Notes

TAKE A WILD GUESS!
BUTTERFLIES USE "THIS" TUBE-LIKE ORGAN TO EXTRACT NECTAR FROM FLOWERS
A) PROBOSCIS
B) TRUMPET
C) VACUUM
D) NECTARCIS

That's A Wild Story!

WRITE A STORY ABOUT TODAY'S NATURE WALK.
OR, HERE'S A WILD IDEA!
BUTTERFLIES ARE POLLINATORS THAT HELP WITH PLANT REPRODUCTION.
WHAT OTHER POLLINATORS CAN YOU THINK OF?

A Walk on the Wild Side

Date: ______________ Time: ______________

Location: ______________________________

Weather:

> I took a walk in the woods and came out taller than the trees.
>
> – Henry David Thoreau

I see:	
I hear:	
I smell:	
I feel:	

Nature Log

Use this space to record something that catches your eye. Sketch, colour, make a leaf rubbing – go wild! Nothing in nature is perfect, so let your inner artist shine.

Field Notes

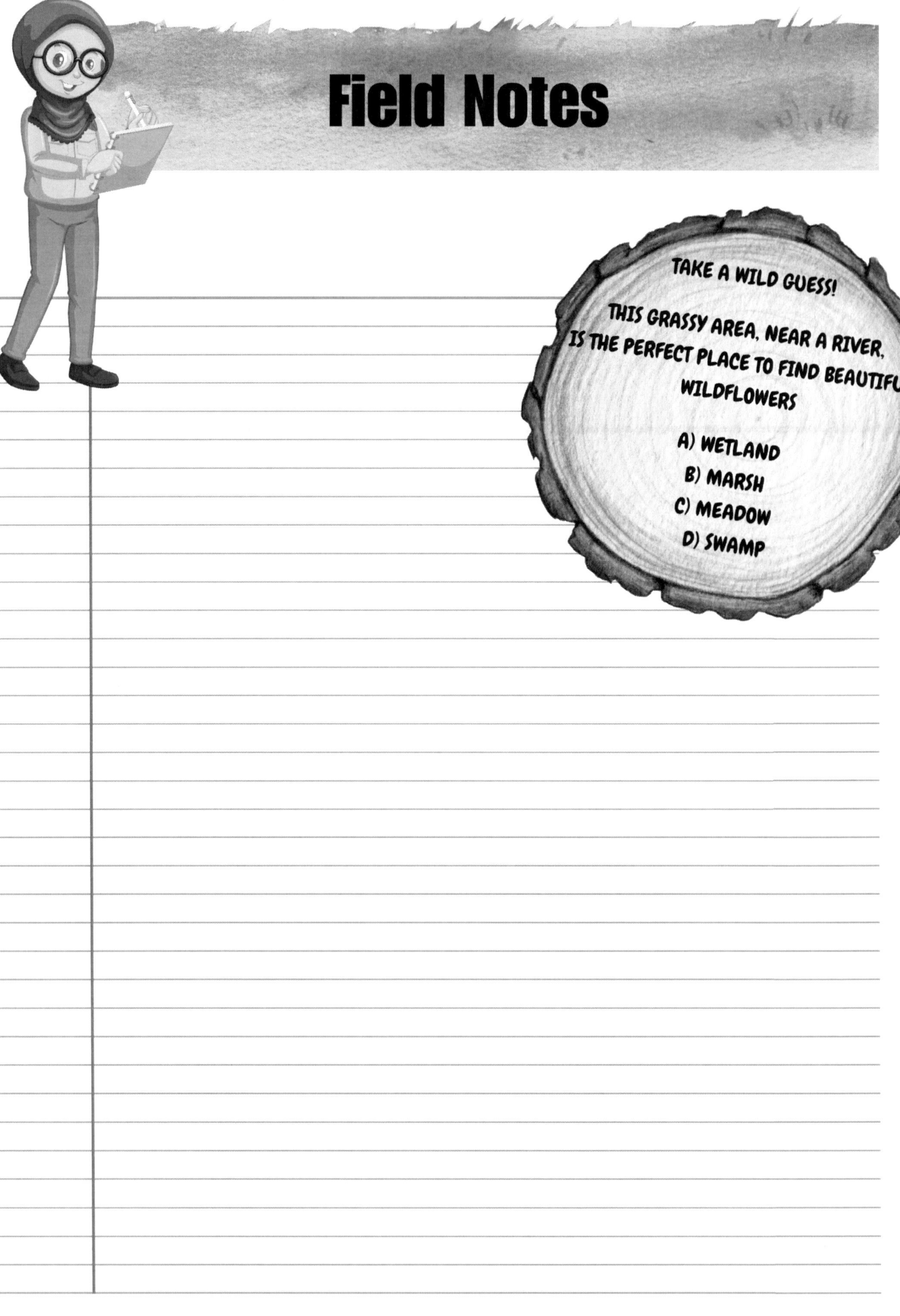
TAKE A WILD GUESS!
THIS GRASSY AREA, NEAR A RIVER, IS THE PERFECT PLACE TO FIND BEAUTIFUL WILDFLOWERS
A) WETLAND
B) MARSH
C) MEADOW
D) SWAMP

That's A Wild Story!

WRITE A STORY ABOUT TODAY'S NATURE WALK.
OR, HERE'S A WILD IDEA!
FOREST, BEACH, MEADOW, OR MOUNTAINS–WHERE DO YOU LIKE TO SPEND TIME IN NATURE, AND WHY?

A Walk on the Wild Side

Date: ______________ Time: ______________

Location: ______________________________

Weather:

> Nature does not hurry, yet everything is accomplished.
>
> – Lao Tzu

I see:	
I hear:	
I smell:	
I feel:	

Nature Log
Use this space to record something that catches your eye.
Sketch, colour, make a leaf rubbing – go wild! Nothing in nature
is perfect, so let your inner artist shine.

Field Notes
TAKE A WILD GUESS!
REPTILES ARE COLD-BLOODED. THEY USE SUNLIGHT OR SHADE TO ADJUST THEIR BODY TEMPERATURE
A) TRUE
B) FALSE

That's A Wild Story!

WRITE A STORY ABOUT TODAY'S NATURE WALK.
OR, HERE'S A WILD IDEA! RESEARCH HOW REPTILES SURVIVE WINTER. USE THIS PAGE TO RECORD WHAT YOU LEARN, AND THEN PRESENT YOUR FACTS TO A FRIEND.

A Walk on the Wild Side

Date: ______________ Time: ______________

Location: ______________________________

Weather:

> Come forth into the light of things, let nature be your teacher.
>
> – William Wordsworth

I see:	
I hear:	
I smell:	
I feel:	

Nature Log

Use this space to record something that catches your eye. Sketch, colour, make a leaf rubbing – go wild! Nothing in nature is perfect, so let your inner artist shine.

Field Notes

TAKE A WILD GUESS!

FAUNA IS THE TERM USED TO DESCRIBE THE ANIMAL LIFE IN A REGION, HABITAT, OR GEOLOGICAL TIME. THE TERM FOR ALL PLANT LIFE IS

A) ANGIOSPERMS
B) GYMNOSPERMS
C) BRYOPHYTES
D) FLORA

That's A Wild Story!

WRITE A STORY ABOUT TODAY'S NATURE WALK.
OR, HERE'S A WILD IDEA! COLLECT A SPECIMEN OF YOUR FAVOURITE FLOWER. LEARN HOW TO PRESS AND PRESERVE PLANTS, AND THEN AFFIX YOUR SPECIMEN TO THIS PAGE.

A Walk on the Wild Side

Date: ______________ **Time:** ______________

Location: ______________________________

Weather:

> To forget how to dig the earth and tend the soil is to forget ourselves.
>
> – Mahatma Gandhi

I see:	
I hear:	
I smell:	
I feel:	

Nature Log

Use this space to record something that catches your eye. Sketch, colour, make a leaf rubbing – go wild! Nothing in nature is perfect, so let your inner artist shine.

Field Notes

TAKE A WILD GUESS!
WHICH IS NOT AN AMPHIBIAN
A) GREAT PLAINS TOAD
B) BLUE-SPOTTED SALAMANDER
C) PAINTED TURTLE
D) ROUGH-SKINNED NEWT

That's A Wild Story!

WRITE A STORY ABOUT TODAY'S NATURE WALK.
OR, HERE'S A WILD IDEA!
DISCUSS AND DRAW TURTLE HABITAT REQUIREMENTS. THINK FOOD, SHELTER, AND BASKING SITES.

A Walk on the Wild Side

Date: ______________ Time: ______________

Location: ______________________________

Weather:

> Leave the roads; take the trails.
>
> - Pythagoras

I see:	
I hear:	
I smell:	
I feel:	

Nature Log

Use this space to record something that catches your eye. Sketch, colour, make a leaf rubbing - go wild! Nothing in nature is perfect, so let your inner artist shine.

Field Notes

TAKE A WILD GUESS!
CANADA'S BOREAL FOREST IS THE WORLD'S LARGEST INTACT FOREST ECOSYSTEM AND CONTAINS 25% OF THE WORLD'S WETLANDS
A) TRUE
B) FALSE

That's A Wild Story!

WRITE A STORY ABOUT TODAY'S NATURE WALK.
OR, HERE'S A WILD IDEA!
USE THIS PAGE TO WRITE DOWN QUESTIONS ABOUT FOREST OR WETLAND ECOSYSTEMS, THEN GO HOME AND DO RESEARCH TO FIND THE ANSWERS.

A Walk on the Wild Side

Date: ____________ Time: ____________

Location: ______________________________

Weather:

> In nature, nothing is perfect, and everything is perfect.
>
> – Alice Walker

I see:	
I hear:	
I smell:	
I feel:	

Nature Log

Use this space to record something that catches your eye.
Sketch, colour, make a leaf rubbing – go wild! Nothing in nature is perfect, so let your inner artist shine.

Field Notes
TAKE A WILD GUESS!
THE REINTRODUCTION OF "THIS" ANIMAL TO YELLOWSTONE NATIONAL PARK INDIRECTLY CHANGED THE FLOW OF RIVERS
A) BEAVER
B) WOLF
C) RIVER OTTER
D) MUSKRAT

That's A Wild Story!

WRITE A STORY ABOUT TODAY'S NATURE WALK.
OR, HERE'S A WILD IDEA!
WRITE DOWN YOUR THEORY ON HOW WOLVES WERE ABLE TO CHANGE THE COURSE OF RIVERS. THE ANSWER INVOLVES THE DOWNSTREAM EFFECTS OF PREDATOR-PREY RELATIONSHIPS.

A Walk on the Wild Side

Date: ______________ Time: ______________

Location: ______________________________

Weather:

> I am glad I will not be young in a future without wilderness.
>
> – Aldo Leopold

I see:	
I hear:	
I smell:	
I feel:	

Nature Log

Use this space to record something that catches your eye. Sketch, colour, make a leaf rubbing – go wild! Nothing in nature is perfect, so let your inner artist shine.

Field Notes

TAKE A WILD GUESS!
UNLIKE DECIDUOUS TREES, CONIFERS LOSE THEIR LEAVES EVERY FALL
A) TRUE
B) FALSE

That's A Wild Story!

WRITE A STORY ABOUT TODAY'S NATURE WALK.
OR, HERE'S A WILD IDEA!
COLLECT A CLUSTER OF PINE NEEDLES, KNOWN AS A FASCICLE, AND A LEAF FROM A DECIDUOUS TREE. COMPARE AND CONTRAST THE TWO.

A Walk on the Wild Side

Date: ____________ Time: ____________

Location: ______________________________

Weather:

"If you truly love nature, you will find beauty everywhere.

– Laura Ingalls Wilder"

I see:	
I hear:	
I smell:	
I feel:	

Nature Log

Use this space to record something that catches your eye. Sketch, colour, make a leaf rubbing – go wild! Nothing in nature is perfect, so let your inner artist shine.

Field Notes

TAKE A WILD GUESS!

THIS ANIMAL HAS THE LARGEST BRAIN OF ALL AVIAN SPECIES. THEY CAN LEARN SPEECH, USE TOOLS, AND HAVE AMAZING MEMORIES

A) BADGER

B) CROW

C) FOX

D) COYOTE

That's A Wild Story!

WRITE A STORY ABOUT TODAY'S NATURE WALK.
OR, HERE'S A WILD IDEA! OBSERVE A GROUP OF CROWS, KNOWN AS A MURDER OF CROWS, AND RECORD BEHAVIOURAL OBSERVATIONS.

Mammal Observation Log

Date	Species	Scientific Name	Quantity	Location

Bird Observation Log

Date	Species	Scientific Name	Quantity	Location

Reptile Observation Log

Date	Species	Scientific Name	Quantity	Location

Date	Species	Scientific Name	Quantity	Location

Plant Observation Log

Date	Species	Scientific Name	Quantity	Location

Insect Observation Log

Date	Species	Scientific Name	Quantity	Location

Field Notes

Field Notes

Field Notes

Field Notes

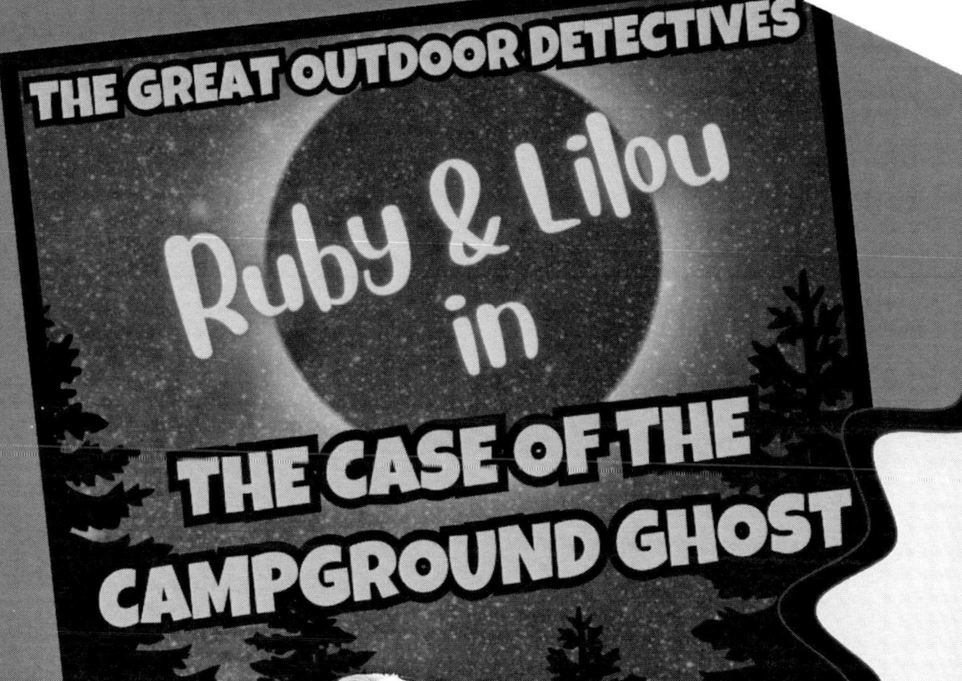

Manufactured by Amazon.ca
Acheson, AB

11842509R00059